Color Me Creative

Kristina Webb

Unlock Your Imagination

HARPER

An Imprint of HarperCollinsPublishers

Library of Congress Control Number: 2015938893

ISBN 978-0-06-241546-2 (trade paperback) — ISBN 978-0-06-244235-2 (special edition)

15 16 17 18 19 PC/RRDC 10 9 8 7 6 5 4 3 2 1

❖

First Edition

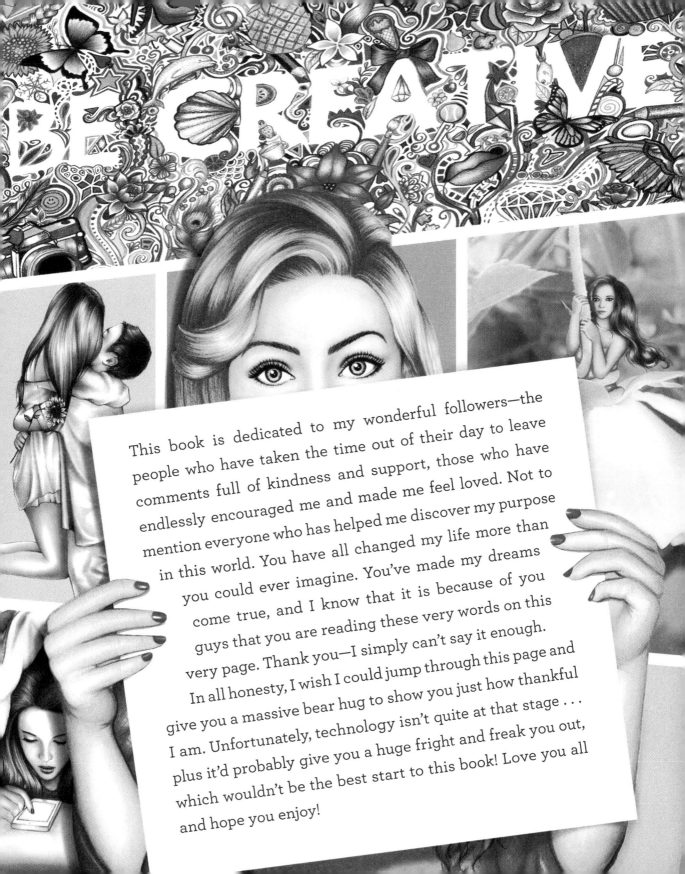

This book is dedicated to my wonderful followers—the people who have taken the time out of their day to leave comments full of kindness and support, those who have endlessly encouraged me and made me feel loved. Not to mention everyone who has helped me discover my purpose in this world. You have all changed my life more than you could ever imagine. You've made my dreams come true, and I know that it is because of you guys that you are reading these very words on this very page. Thank you—I simply can't say it enough. In all honesty, I wish I could jump through this page and give you a massive bear hug to show you just how thankful I am. Unfortunately, technology isn't quite at that stage . . . plus it'd probably give you a huge fright and freak you out, which wouldn't be the best start to this book! Love you all and hope you enjoy!

Contents

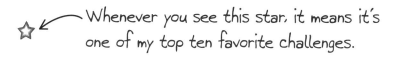

☆ Whenever you see this star, it means it's one of my top ten favorite challenges.

☐ ← Use these boxes below to mark which challenges you've completed.

Unbound App

Unlock exclusive, never-before-seen videos from Kristina. . . . This book features multimedia content beyond the printed page. Some of the pages in this edition of *Color Me Creative* feature a special icon you can use to activate and discover additional content on your smartphone, mobile device, or tablet device.

HOW DOES IT WORK?

1. Visit www.harpercollinsunbound.com to download the free app for your iOS or Android device.

2. When you see this icon  on pages throughout the book, open the app on your device and scan the page.

3. The app will do the rest, bringing multimedia and interactive content that relates to the page you're reading right onto your device.

A Little Bit About Me

My story begins in the very small yet beautiful country of New Zealand. I was born on September 8, 1995, in the city of Tauranga. My entrance into the world didn't go all that smoothly. According to my mom, it took a little while for me to figure out how to breathe, and within seconds I was turning a lovely shade of blue, which is always a great start to life! The nurses rushed off to fix me and I was returned to my mother shortly after, no longer resembling a blueberry. Apparently, I cried so much at the hospital that my mom ended up getting her own private room for the entire week, which she really appreciated (you're welcome, Mom).

After a wonderful week in that private hospital room I was taken home to meet my very energetic three-year-old sister, Rochelle, to start my role in life as her new "toy."

Tauranga

Baby Kristina

Real thing!

Baby doll

Prior to me being born, my parents had purchased Rochelle a very realistic baby doll, but no, that just wouldn't do. She wanted the real thing and did NOT like to share!

Thankfully, Rochelle had some very strict rules with this new "toy" of hers. She was only allowed to hold me if she was sitting down and being supervised. However, being the little troublemaker that she was, a short time later she got a bit bored with these rules and decided to take me on a little "sister bonding" adventure in the backyard. My mom witnessed Rochelle running around on the lawn with me, tripping, falling, and dropping me. Naturally I started crying, which must have freaked her out because she left me lying in the grass while she ran inside, locking all the doors behind her. This was the first of many times Rochelle locked me out. She obviously had a strong desire to go back to being an only child!

Despite my lovely big sister's best efforts (she loves me, really!), I survived my first two years in New Zealand. But nothing could have prepared me for the adventure that lay ahead. Next stop, Vanuatu!

More sister "bonding"

New Zealand

FUN FACTS

• When I say New Zealand is small, I'm not kidding around! It is much smaller than the state of California and has a population of roughly 4.5 million people.

• New Zealand has a lot of sheep, like, A LOT of them. There are around seven sheep for each person. Not that we all walk around with seven sheep on a leash or anything, but you get what I mean.

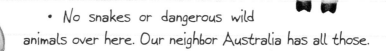

• New Zealand is the first country in the world to begin each new day; therefore we are the first to bring in the New Year. (We're in the future!)

• No snakes or dangerous wild animals over here. Our neighbor Australia has all those.

• New Zealand is well known for being the breathtaking location where the Lord of the Rings movies were filmed. The location of the hobbits' homes is a forty-five-minute drive from where I was born.

Giving my nan a mischievous look. Haha!

Just some
casual reading

The Island Life

At two years old I had my first overseas experience. My parents were both offered pharmacist jobs in the tropical Pacific island town of Port Vila, Vanuatu, and within a couple of months our house was rented, cars were sold, and I was on my very first airplane.

When we landed in Vanuatu I was covered in chicken pox (something my mom discovered I had halfway through the flight!). We then arrived at our new home to the buzzing of mosquitos and giant moths. Bitten and itchy was not an ideal way to start my new "tropical paradise" lifestyle.

Aside from the mosquitos there were also noisy frogs in the neighbor's pool, squeaky geckos on our ceilings, huge land crabs scratching at our ranchsliders (sliding doors) in the middle of the night, and wild dogs chasing us every time we ventured out of our front gate. At first, our new home didn't exactly resemble the pictures painted in all the travel brochures.

Scary is definitely a word I would use to describe our first few weeks in Vanuatu. There were bare-chested men with huge knives constantly walking the streets by our house. One day, one of these men walked up our driveway toward me. I was absolutely terrified (as to be expected) and did what any sane toddler would do. . . . I hid under my bed crying. My mom later found me and showed me that the man was simply cutting our lawn with his machete. His name was Frank and he was our gardener. Frank actually became a great friend of mine, who I would often "help" in the garden, picking flowers and making fairy rings.

There were many ways in which Port Vila life was different from our life in New Zealand. We were used to a home with smooth roads, strict traffic rules, clean supermarkets, satellite TV, and a cool moderate climate. We had traded all this for oven-like temperatures, riding around in the back of our pickup truck along pothole-covered roads, and witnessing whole families sleeping under their produce tables at the local markets as chickens wandered around them.

Mom

Rochelle's happy face

Despite the many challenges, I eventually learned that there was a lot to love about Vanuatu! Most important, Vanuatu was where I first started drawing!

My mom was teaching Rochelle how to create her own paper dolls. And being that annoying little sister who wanted to do everything my big sister did . . . I joined in. From that day forward I've never stopped creating. I became obsessed, drawing on anything, anywhere, and anytime! I was also one of those little girls who loved anything to do with fairy tales and princesses—to the point where I legitimately convinced myself I was an actual princess. There was a time when I refused to wear anything but my long princess dresses for months in the unbearable heat.

Drawing I did at two years old

11

Playing princesses

12

With my love for fairy tales and all things magical came my interest in books, and in particular, picture books. I would sit for hours staring at the stunning illustrations of fairies and mermaids, my imagination running wild! I started to incorporate what I saw on the beautiful pages of those books into my own drawings, giving my paper dolls elaborate dresses with frills, bows, and shimmering wings. Drawing swept me away into my own little world. I created my own characters and stories, getting lost in it all.

When I wasn't caught up in my own fantasy world, I spent my days snorkeling through colorful schools of fish. I learned how to climb palm trees for coconuts, jumped off waterfalls, explored the tropical jungle often carried on the shoulders of local friends, and ran barefoot on the white sand beaches. I particularly loved finding hermit crabs with my sister and making them race each other.

I attended the local preschool, and you could say that I stood out a

little. I remember sitting on a mat and listening to the teacher while the kids behind me pulled my hair. My mom explained to me that they did this to see if it was real. Many of the people who lived on the island had never seen blond hair before and were fascinated.

After living in Vanuatu for a few years, I became accustomed to this way of life and thought it was "normal." I figured this was how most people in the world lived. Little did I know that I was about to discover just how wrong I was. I was about to enter the next chapter of my life. We were on the move again, and this time the destination was Gold Coast, Australia.

Vanuatu=Paradise

My favorite spot,
Hideaway Island

G'day, Mate!

GOLD COAST

Australia was like another world to my five-year-old self. The palm trees that I was so used to seeing everywhere were suddenly replaced with tall buildings that seemed to disappear into the clouds. The high-rises weren't the only difference. It was here that I was enrolled in my first proper school and was introduced to formal education. Embarrassing as it is, I actually had to repeat preschool! How does one fail preschool, you may ask? Well, apparently what I had learned previously in Vanuatu wasn't advanced enough. I guess you need to know

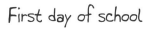

First day of school

Kritina

the alphabet and the sounds of the letters in order to start school.

A year older than everyone in my class, I walked into school and it was love at first sight—with the art corner, that is. I can only describe it as the most beautiful thing I had ever laid eyes on and from that day forward we were inseparable. I practically lived in that corner and it was also how I made my first Australian friends. My fellow classmates would stand around watching me paint and draw while arguing over who would get the art when I was finished!

At my mom's first parent-teacher conference, my teacher told her that I could barely write my own name, but I could draw like a teenager. Unlike what some parents might have done, my mom didn't freak out and confiscate my pencils in the hopes of turning me into an academic daughter. Instead she decided that from that day forward she would do everything she could to support me and my love for creating. This is something that I can't thank her enough for.

Oh, and don't worry, I did eventually learn how to write my own name too, just in case you were wondering.

Despite my love for the art corner, this was the first time in my life that I had ever experienced how strict and structured life really could be. I found it so difficult to sit still and be confined to a classroom for hours on end. Looking back, I'm sure my classmates thought I was slightly strange, as my teacher would constantly be telling me to put my shoes back on. I was just so used to running around barefoot and carefree. It probably didn't help that my mom used to pack me some really unique, healthy lunches too. I can vividly recall one little girl telling me that my whole-grain crackers looked like a wasps' nest. So of course, in return I informed her that her delicious chocolate yogurt looked like a poo. Hey, I was five. . . . It was the best I had!

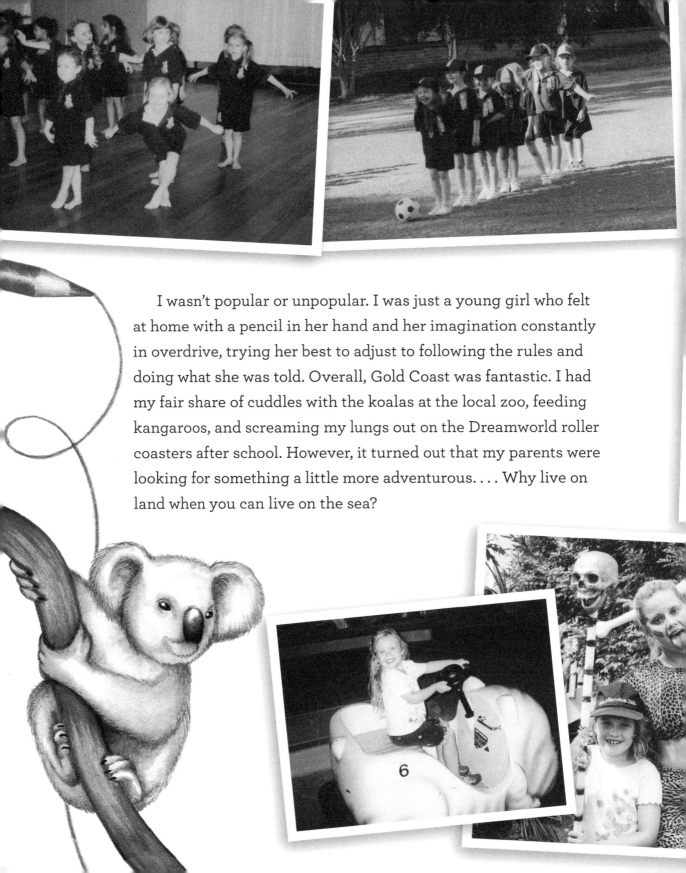

I wasn't popular or unpopular. I was just a young girl who felt at home with a pencil in her hand and her imagination constantly in overdrive, trying her best to adjust to following the rules and doing what she was told. Overall, Gold Coast was fantastic. I had my fair share of cuddles with the koalas at the local zoo, feeding kangaroos, and screaming my lungs out on the Dreamworld roller coasters after school. However, it turned out that my parents were looking for something a little more adventurous. . . . Why live on land when you can live on the sea?

Sailing the Days Away

Living on the sea, Kristina? What are you talking about? Well, lovely people, that was the moment I realized that I was indeed . . . a mermaid!

Okay, well, not really, but how cool would that have been? My real answer is that my parents decided to buy a boat. Now, this boat wasn't just any boat; it was a yacht. It wasn't just any yacht either. It was our official new home for the next few years. We were pulled out of school as fast as we had been enrolled, which, I think, is every seven-year-old's dream come true!

Sadly that dream was short-lived, as I was told we were driving to Brisbane to register Rochelle and me for home school. Our new home was what you call a Trailer Sailor, which means it was just big enough to live in yet small enough to attach to the back of your car and tow. We towed our floating house to Airlie Beach, pushed it into the water, and set off sailing around a stunning group of islands called the Whitsundays.

Now, I want you to stop reading for a second and get out that list of places you want to visit before you die. (I know you have one, and if not . . . don't worry! I've started one to inspire you on the next page.) Now, write a big WHITSUNDAYS at the top of it. Trust me on this. You'll thank me later, and if you need further reassurance, then Google the place; it's breathtaking.

We spent our days sailing from one island to another, each one more beautiful than the last. After doing

26

PLACES TO VISIT BEFORE I DIE

Scan this!

1.

2.

3.

4.

5.

6.

7.

8.

9.

10.

our schoolwork during the days at sea, we would often jump off the side of the boat and snorkel our way through our lunch breaks. On our weekends we would anchor and explore new islands. Many of them had luxury resorts where my parents would organize a deal with the hotel to let us swim in the pools and for Rochelle and me to attend the kids' clubs. The thing with home school is that it can be harder to interact with people of your own age. These kids' clubs allowed us to make new friends. Even though we would often be saying good-bye to them a few days later when their holidays were over, my mom knew it was important that we socialized like we would have done if we were in traditional school. In my opinion home school was perfect and I ended up moving up a year, which actually moved me into the year where I was sup-posed to be in the first place. (Remember the whole failing-preschool thing?) I think some of the reasons I loved home school are that I could learn things at my own pace and that I had that one-on-one attention from my teacher (Mom) when I needed help, which was so valuable.

Being able to have the freedom to do little things, like eating when I was hungry and going to the bathroom with-out having to ask, made me feel so much more in control of everything, and basically

Lunch break!

Sunset sailing!

just happy. If there's anything I've learned it's that when you're happy you produce your best work. On the right is an example of one of my home school papers where I had to draw my surroundings.

We would go to sleep when the sun set and wake up when it rose, living day to day carefree by our own rules, and exploring and discovering new and exciting places each day. Cruising around the Whitsundays wasn't always smooth sailing. But my parents wanted adventure and that's what we got.

One time my older sister accidentally put my art homework a little too close to the stove while making pancakes for breakfast.

That resulted in a fire on board, which is never a good thing, especially when it comes to boats. We managed to put it out, but it's safe to say it took her a while before she made pancakes again, and it taught me not to leave my art anywhere near her.

Another time we were woken up by a loud thud to find out that our anchor had dragged, causing us to crash into

6 **Look at** your "snapshot" for natural and built features. **List** them in the columns where they belong.

Natural features	Built features
Trees	
Water	
Grass	
Sky	

Wow! You are lucky to have such a beautiful natural environment

a nearby boat—not the most neighborly thing for us to do. It wasn't the only time our anchor dragged either. A few weeks later we woke once again, this time to a loud scraping sound as we smashed into some unforgiving rocks at low tide and our precious home got stuck! I remember watching sleepily as my parents quickly jumped into the water in their pajamas to push the boat away from danger. Looking back now, we should probably have gotten a heavier anchor!

Oh! And there was also that time I almost drowned after a game of "tackling each other off the boat" with my sister. To cut a long story short, I lost the game and found myself underwater. When I tried to resurface I kept hitting my head on the bottom of the boat. Naturally panic kicked in as I realized I was trapped. I can tell you now it's not fun being trapped underwater desperately needing to breathe, and at the time being a mermaid would have really come in handy. It was all very dramatic as I gave up struggling and started sinking to the bottom of the sea. This was when Rochelle must have decided she wanted a sister after

Exploring in our dinghy

all and dived in, grabbed my disappearing foot, and pulled me up. I'm pretty sure she saved my life that day, but she also pushed me in. So they sort of even each other out.

Of course, you can't live on a boat in Australia without having at least one run-in with a crocodile. One beautiful day we were fishing in a swamp in a blow-up dinghy, minding our own business and peacefully floated over a large log. Yep, you guessed it, not a log after all. We realized this when the log opened its eyes. I don't think you can understand the full meaning of the word terror until you are literally a few feet away from a crocodile in a blow-up (yes, that's right, *blow-up*) dinghy. Thankfully the "log" didn't seem too hungry as it watched us slowly paddle away, then quickly turn on our 5 HP motor (which wasn't much faster than using the paddles!).

I think the biggest shock of all, though, was when an enormous fifty-foot humpback whale and its baby surfaced beside us while we were casually eating our breakfast on deck. They were giants swimming around our little twenty-six-foot boat and they gave us a brilliant yet terrifying display.

Satisfied with these adventures and surprisingly still alive, my parents decided that it was time for Rochelle to get back into regular school since she was nearing high-school age. Our boat was sold and we relocated back to where it all began . . . New Zealand.

Dear Mum
I Love you
im sorry
im not
well enogh
to do
math

← Apparently I was too sick to do math but well enough to draw. I've got my priorities straight. Haha!

Kiwis Fly Home

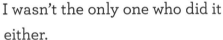

When we arrived in New Zealand we decided to move back to where I was brought into this world, Tauranga.

At nine years old, I knew my days of home school were over when my mom handed me a uniform that seemed to be from the Middle Ages. The skirt was so long it was a tripping hazard. However, the length proved to have its advantages on those cold wintery days I walked to school with my cozy pajama pants hidden underneath. No one ever knew . . . and I'm fairly positive I wasn't the only one who did it either.

It was impossible to find a photo of me in that uniform—pretty sure I tried to destroy them all. But I went back to the school uniform shop and put it back on just for you guys. If you're ever having a bad day just remember that I had to wear this for seven years of my life, and I give you permission to have a good giggle about it.

Hideous uniforms aside, the next few years flew by. It was

nice to be settled in one place and close to family again. I had missed my nan and pop so much after living overseas for such a long time. School wasn't too bad either. I made a nice group of friends; was a sheep in the school play; got my first pet, an adorable ginger kitten called Cookie; and life was good.

I was known as that girl who did crazy art and didn't talk all that much—at least in public anyway. (When I was with my friends you couldn't shut me up!) I wasn't necessarily

"cool" in school but I had my group of friends and that's all that mattered. Funnily enough, whenever there was a group project that involved art I suddenly seemed to become the most popular girl in the class.

Nan

From ten to twelve years old everything was easy, life was easy. I passed everything with flying colors and received too many certificates and awards to count (goody-goody alert). In the last year of primary, when I was eleven years old, I was nominated for the Writers' Cup and ended up winning the Mathematics Cup for the top girl student in the school. Nothing says *nerd* like winning the Math Cup, but hey, I owned that title. If anyone is calling you a nerd, you should own it too. It's a compliment: they're calling you smart. There is absolutely NOTHING wrong with doing well.

MATH

Nerd! :)

I was slightly obsessed with my sister's and my new kittens!

Taking Cookie for a little stroll!

A New Beginning

It was during middle school that my whole world came crashing down. Well, in the eyes of my twelve-year-old self anyway. My mom and sister had been away in Auckland for the weekend and picked me up from a sleepover on their way home.

I don't think I'll ever forget the moment my mom unlocked the front door to find a half-empty house. My dad was gone, just like that. He left us and never came back.

Those first few weeks weren't easy, and it seemed like it was just us three girls against the world for a while there. I can vividly remember a week after he left when my school held a dance that all the Year Eight students and their parents attended. It was all going okay until one of the teachers announced through the microphone that it was time for a father-daughter dance.

I watched in what seemed like slow motion as my friends walked toward their smiling dads, who looked down at them with so much love in their eyes, and I just broke. I couldn't stay in that room for another second, and ran into the bathroom, locked myself away, and cried.

Looking back now I wish I had just confidently grabbed my mom's hand and pulled her onto that dance floor. She was a mom AND a dad to me from then on and she had more than enough love in her heart to play both roles. As I have gotten older I've begun to realize that so many people don't have two parents. What is most important is to hold on to the person who actually does play that role in your life. Blood isn't that important—it's about who is there for you, who is interested in you, and who will always help you when you need it.

The divorce was a messy one that went on for a long time. My mom went back to her family's last name of Webb and Rochelle was old enough to legally change hers as well. They were both Webbs and I was stuck with a last name that no longer felt right. I wasn't old enough to change it without both parents' permission, but after months of begging, my dad finally signed the papers and I became Kristina Webb.

It felt like a brand-new family, a fresh start. A family I knew was unbreakable, no matter what. We three girls now have a bond that can make it through anything, and it only grows stronger with each year that goes by. My mom and my sister, these two incredible women, have made everything possible for me, and they are still right by my side every step of the way.

With my new last name came a new person, a stronger person. I found a way to channel all my emotions and feelings into my art and it was the escape I so desperately needed.

Art vs. Everything Else

hen I hit those early teen years, and, as I'm sure many of you know, they are a whole other level of complicated. The more stressful school got, the more I lost myself in my own world of art. I didn't even realize I was doing it a lot of the time. If there was a pen or paper nearby, then I couldn't help but draw and everything else just faded away. Classes dragged on and on and I think one of my problems was that I knew what I wanted to do and I couldn't wait to get on with it. I just wanted to do art; why did I need science? How was knowing how many electrons are in an atom going to help me in life?

School worksheet

Inside schoolbook

It's safe to say my science and math books were completely covered in doodles that drove my teachers crazy but that my mom wanted to frame.

I took every art class I could possibly take, but once in those classes I began to resent just how little control we had over what we were creating. We were told exactly what to do, how to do it, and what materials to use. I didn't feel like there was any room for creativity or original ideas in those classes. I can recall being told to study artists from the past for inspiration and to copy their styles. I was interested and fascinated with their work, but as far as copying their styles—why? I wanted to create my own style.

I learned very quickly that if you want good grades you give the art teachers exactly what they want—it just didn't feel right to me. In my opinion there is no wrong or right with art—art is art.

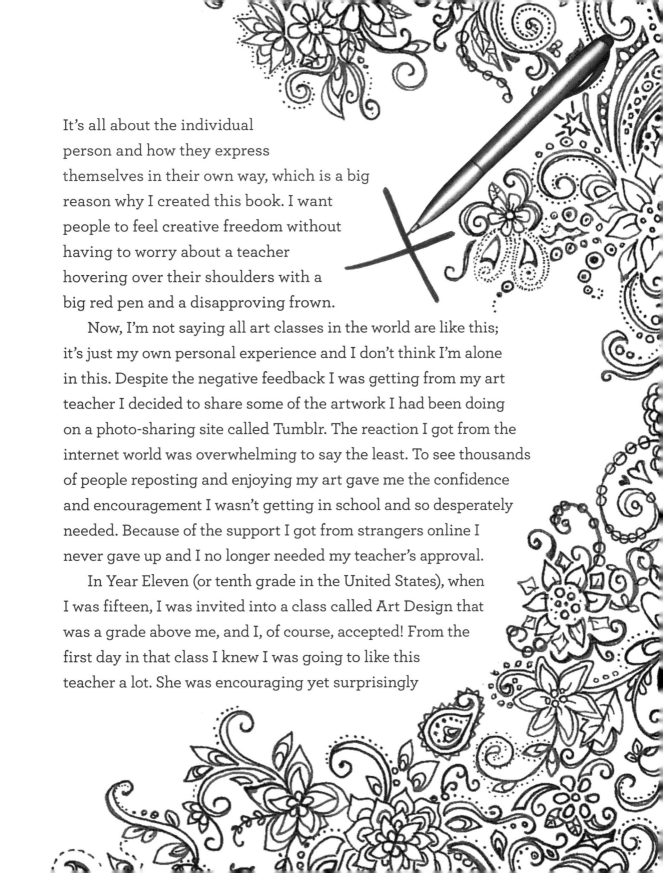

It's all about the individual person and how they express themselves in their own way, which is a big reason why I created this book. I want people to feel creative freedom without having to worry about a teacher hovering over their shoulders with a big red pen and a disapproving frown.

Now, I'm not saying all art classes in the world are like this; it's just my own personal experience and I don't think I'm alone in this. Despite the negative feedback I was getting from my art teacher I decided to share some of the artwork I had been doing on a photo-sharing site called Tumblr. The reaction I got from the internet world was overwhelming to say the least. To see thousands of people reposting and enjoying my art gave me the confidence and encouragement I wasn't getting in school and so desperately needed. Because of the support I got from strangers online I never gave up and I no longer needed my teacher's approval.

In Year Eleven (or tenth grade in the United States), when I was fifteen, I was invited into a class called Art Design that was a grade above me, and I, of course, accepted! From the first day in that class I knew I was going to like this teacher a lot. She was encouraging yet surprisingly hands-off, letting the students explore their own creativity in their own ways.

This wonderful teacher introduced me to the magic of scanning my drawings into a computer. It blew my mind! It was the start of a whole new artistic world for me, with endless possibilities. After this amazing discovery, I used my savings to buy a laptop with Adobe Photoshop. I was completely hooked. I got more excited the more I taught myself how to use the tools and effects.

Over the summer holidays I worked on new drawings almost every day and uploaded them to my Tumblr account as often as possible. I had gained around ten thousand followers by then, which was absolute craziness to me! One of the drawings I had done earlier in the year went viral on the internet with over three hundred thousand notes. I began to see it everywhere, from Facebook pages to websites to hanging up in people's homes. It became one of the most well-known drawings on Tumblr and was recognized by teenagers all over the world. With all the support from these followers plus their amazing responses, I knew I wanted to do this for the rest of my life.

But what I will truly never forget is the first message I got saying that I had inspired someone to start drawing. I think that this is one of the biggest compliments an artist can ever receive. It really affected me to think that I had made an impact on this person's life, that because of ME they were inspired to draw and to create things.

That's when I realized what I wanted my life's purpose to be. I wanted to inspire as many people as possible in my lifetime, whether that meant inspiring them to start drawing, get back into art after a long time, think in a more creative way, express their emotions through art, or figure out their passions and chase their dreams. Knowing you've had an impact on someone's life, improved it, or helped them through something is the most rewarding feeling in the world.

Art board for school I
did at sixteen years old
(I think I may have liked
the color purple.)

A Different Way to Learn

Having discovered my life's purpose at fifteen, I then doodled my way through the required classes, counting down the seconds on the clock until that school bell rang and I could finally race home to share a new drawing online. Every morning when my alarm went off it seemed harder and harder to crawl out of bed. The only thing that kept me motivated was the fact that I didn't want to miss my Art Design class and I wanted to see my friends. As I grew more and more frustrated with the system, my teachers grew more frustrated with me. Eventually we came to an arrangement with the school that I could take subjects like English, science, and math via home school and just attend art classes at the campus.

It worked out perfectly—it was a situation where I still got to spend time with my friends during lunch and stay

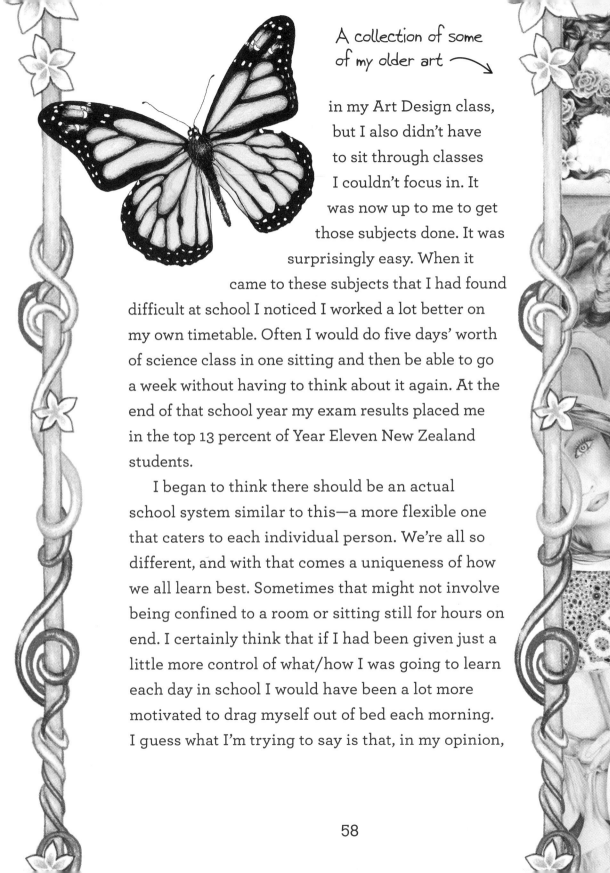

in my Art Design class, but I also didn't have to sit through classes I couldn't focus in. It was now up to me to get those subjects done. It was surprisingly easy. When it came to these subjects that I had found difficult at school I noticed I worked a lot better on my own timetable. Often I would do five days' worth of science class in one sitting and then be able to go a week without having to think about it again. At the end of that school year my exam results placed me in the top 13 percent of Year Eleven New Zealand students.

I began to think there should be an actual school system similar to this—a more flexible one that caters to each individual person. We're all so different, and with that comes a uniqueness of how we all learn best. Sometimes that might not involve being confined to a room or sitting still for hours on end. I certainly think that if I had been given just a little more control of what/how I was going to learn each day in school I would have been a lot more motivated to drag myself out of bed each morning. I guess what I'm trying to say is that, in my opinion,

Life is Beautiful

Love

Kristina Webb

UNLOCK THE CREATIVITY

Work I created for
my Art Design class

ideally there would be a system that gives people more freedom in their lives instead of just placing everyone into the same box to do the same thing every day. I realize it would be hard to manage a system like this, but it's worth putting the idea out there to explore.

Unfortunately, regardless of the fantastic results, the school informed me that our arrangement couldn't go on in 2012. I was at a loss over what to do. I considered ending my school years there and enrolling in a university for art at sixteen years old, and even went so far as to spend a day in a graphic design course to see what it was like. I quickly realized I wasn't ready for that. I felt too young and the course didn't seem quite right. My mom and I continued searching for alternatives and one day my sister said, "You could move to another country." Unsure as to whether this was her next attempt to get rid of me, I gave her a questioning look and she continued to explain, "No, seriously, you love traveling. Why don't you do a high school exchange program?" We all paused for a minute, then raced for the laptop to begin researching which exciting countries I could go to.

So many countries to choose from!

2008

2012

2010

2008

2009

2012

My Teenage Years

2011

Hello, USA!

After considering different options, I quickly fell in love with the idea of going to high school in the United States. My mind was already picturing it—the yellow school buses, cafeterias, dances like homecoming and prom. It was going to be just like the movies. I could already tell this was going to be the experience of a lifetime.

Before I knew it I was enrolled in an exchange program, my bags were packed, and I was on a thirteen-hour flight to a country I had never been to, to live with a family I had never met. I was surprisingly calm about the whole thing, even though I almost lost my passport, was close to missing my connecting flight from San Francisco to New York, and then found out I had left my new camera on the plane. The whole trip lasted thirty hours before I finally reached my destination, Boston.

It was there that I and three hundred other students from around the world attended Culture Camp. We all had one thing in common: we were about to get

Flying into America! →

the American high school experience. The camp was all about preparing us for American culture and the what-to-dos and the what-not-to-dos. The ten or so New Zealanders at the camp were the only ones who spoke English as their first language so we also sat through two weeks of classes double-checking we knew how to say things such as *T-shirt* and *bathroom*. This resulted in us Kiwis (people from New Zealand) being at the top of the class, but I guess you could say we had an unfair advantage. . . .

After making a whole lot of new friends from all over the world I boarded yet another plane to head to my new home for the next year. When I chose to go to the United States I had no say in which state I would actually live in—it was up to a family to pick me, and that's where I'd go. I was chosen by a wonderful family of three who lived in Grand Rapids, Michigan.

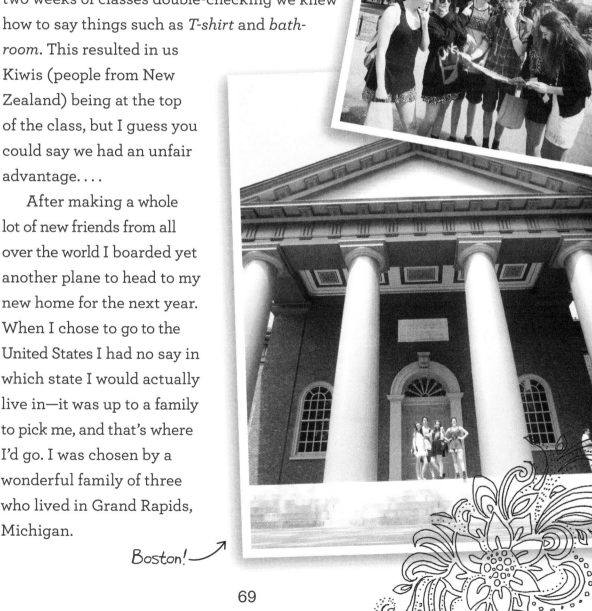

Kiwis!

Boston!

69

My awesome
host family!

Waiting for me at the airport
with a video camera and a big
bunch of sunflowers was my
host family, who instantly treated me as one of their own.

After straining to fit my rather large luggage into the car's
boot (oh, that's right, Americans call it a trunk!), we all hopped in
the car.

I remember silently freaking out as my host mom, who was
sitting on the right-hand side of the car in the front, kept turning
around to talk to me. In my exhausted state I had forgotten that
in America the driver is seated on the left-hand side. I remember
thinking to myself, *Oh my gosh . . . this crazy lady needs to keep
her eyes on the road!* The concern must have shown on my face
as she asked me if I was okay. It was then I realized she wasn't

in fact driving, and they all had a good laugh about it. On the way we stopped for some frozen yogurt, something I had never experienced before . . . and let me tell you, frozen yogurt is an experience, all right. I knew I was going to like these people.

We drove until there were only dirt roads and trees surrounding us in every direction. The car turned and started to drive up what looked like another street, but I was told it was their driveway. It was beautiful. We were right in the middle of a forest and my host mom told me you could sometimes see deer running through the gaps in the trees. Once inside they gave me a tour of the house, then opened the door to a room they had decorated especially for me. Even pictures of my family and friends from back in New Zealand had been printed, framed, and placed by my bed. I felt like the luckiest exchange student in the world to have been welcomed into this family's home so warmly.

Through my host family, I finally got the little sister I had always dreamed of. She was ten years old and the best way to describe her would be energetic and full of life. There was never a dull moment when she was around; there was also never a moment she wasn't cartwheeling or dancing around the room with her extremely contagious smile. My host dad was an unbelievable singer and my host mom was an extremely caring and kind school counselor (she always knew how to cheer me up when I started to feel homesick). Within a week I felt like I had been living in that house my whole life, and although we all spoke the same language we quickly discovered that there were still some big differences in our terminology that kept us all laughing.

We actually made a list.

Differences

New Zealand	United States
Boot of a car	Trunk of a car
Rubbish	Trash
Petrol	Gas
Lolly	Candy
Dairy	Convenience Store
Togs	Swimsuits
Biscuit	Cookie
Jandals	Flip-Flops
Rubber	Eraser
Cutlery	Utensils
Tap	Faucet
Tramping	Hiking
Full Stop	Period (I don't think I'll ever understand this one. Doesn't full stop make so much more sense?!)

The Bean in Chicago!

In the days leading up to school my host family kept me busy taking me on the most wonderful outings to the lake, theme parks, and even a road trip to Chicago, showing me as much as they possibly could and completely inviting me into their lives. I especially remember the day they took me to the local zoo and they stared at me in disbelief as they watched their weird exchange student squeal and freak out every time she saw a squirrel or chipmunk and chase after them with her camera. I guess it probably did look a little funny, being in front of a tiger's cage with my camera pointed toward something so common to Americans as a cute fluffy squirrel.

Beautiful Lake Michigan

Squirrel!

The day my alarm started beeping at five thirty a.m. I thought it was some kind of cruel joke (I am NO morning person). I then realized it was my first day of high school! I raced down the long driveway and did a little happy dance inside as I saw the yellow bus roll its way toward me. School wasn't exactly how movies like *Mean Girls* make it out to be. Everyone was actually extremely friendly to the new girl with the strange accent, and it was so interesting to see how different school was there. As an exchange student, I was allowed more flexibility, so I got to choose my subjects and opted out of science and math, taking subjects such as photography, drawing, sculpture, and AP Art. I attended the football games with my new friends and cheered from the sidelines along with

everyone else, having no real idea what was actually going on. Pretty soon everyone was shopping for homecoming dresses and my new friends and I were all dancing the night away in our too-high heels. I was right about one thing for sure: this exchange program was the experience of a lifetime.

My Instagram account was born the same day I was, or seventeen years later anyway. That's right, on September 8 for my seventeenth birthday in Michigan, I was given my first iPhone. I was given it in a rather creative way as well, which seemed fitting. My host family took me out to lunch and before I knew it they all started singing "Happy Birthday" as a waitress walked toward me with a tray and an upside-down bowl, which I assumed was hiding a slice of cake. I took the bowl off and embarrassingly screamed loudly as I saw not cake, but an iPhone. I had been wanting one for years and an iPhone is probably the only thing that could've been under that bowl that beats cake. Because . . . cake. YUM!

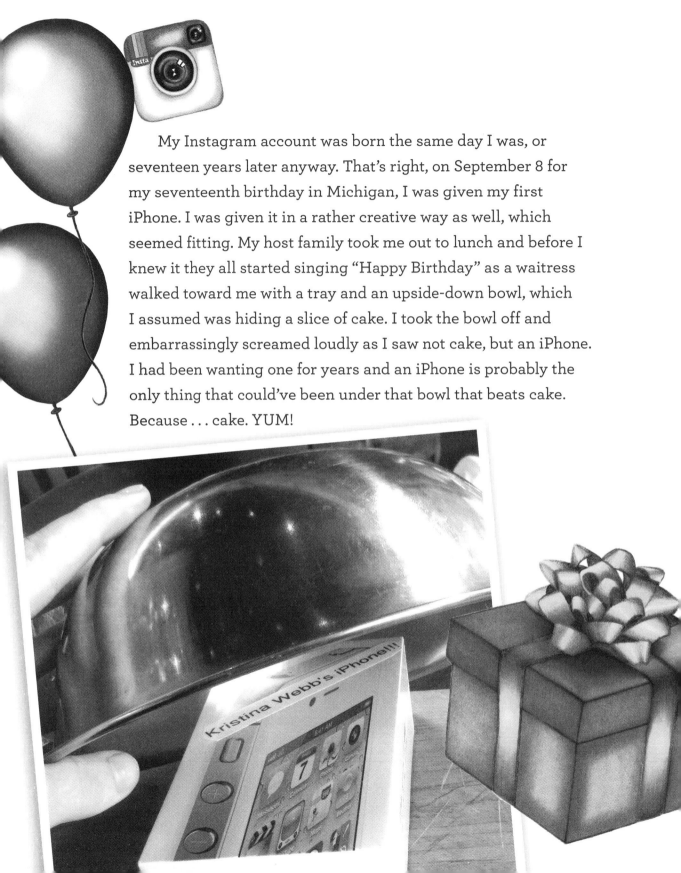

It wasn't even so much wanting an iPhone as wanting the ability to have an Instagram account so that I could finally start @colour_me_creative. The minute I set up my new phone I went straight to the app store and downloaded Instagram, already planning what my first post would be. I was beyond excited to start sharing my art on a whole new platform. As I was learning how the app worked, I came across one of my drawings on the popular page. Confused, I pressed it and saw that an account with a large following had posted it. I commented a nice *Thank you for posting my drawing* and to my surprise the account responded, telling me that they would be happy to repost it with credit, and they did just that. My account grew to over sixteen thousand followers in just a few days and soon enough I was making the popular page on my own.

That was when I knew my dream of inspiring people had really taken off. I made it my mission to post a new drawing at least once a day and before I knew it, even celebrities started taking notice. I'll never forget the day Keegan Allen (Toby from *Pretty Little Liars*) commented, followed, reposted, and then made

I eventually got to meet Ed Sheeran in person and give him the picture I'd drawn of him!

one of my drawings his profile picture for a few months. Once he had noticed my art, other celebrities started to as well, such as Chloë Moretz, Tyra Banks, Lauren Conrad, Bethany Mota, Ed Sheeran, Ariana Grande, Cody Simpson, and Peyton List, to name a few.

At this point many of my followers were asking me to draw them. I decided the best way to give back to all these supportive, lovely people was to have a hashtag called #drawmekristina, with which they could tag their own photos, and I would choose one a week at random to draw. This ended up working incredibly well. Surprising the follower I drew and hopefully making their day was the highlight of my week.

Over time, when I typed my username into the search bar I started to notice accounts made especially to honor my artwork and me. It was so strange—I was just an ordinary girl who practically lived in her pajamas with her hair piled on top of her head in some sort of crazy bun who liked to draw lying on the floor and share what she created.

There just wasn't enough time in the day for me to do all the drawings I wanted to do. Throw schoolwork in there too and I had big problems. I tried my best to balance the two but art always seemed to win. When you're an exchange student, you have to keep up certain grades to be able to stay in the United States and my grades were slipping, FAST. Around that time my grades weren't the only thing plummeting to the ground. As winter hit, snow covered everything in sight, and let me tell you, winter in

Michigan is INTENSE. I had never experienced anything like it. I had seen snow before but only on mountains—having snow in your backyard is a whole other story.

The first day I woke up to the white wonderland outside I got so excited I ran out the door and face-planted on the ground. The excitement began to wear off the colder it got and the earlier I had to get up. Forcing myself to walk out of the cozy, warm house into the pitch dark so early in the morning to step into what

I can only describe as Antarctica was a battle. Once outside I had another battle to face in trying not to slip as I walked (half ran because I was always late for the bus) down that long, icy driveway. I swear I was on my bum more often than my feet. Oh, and don't even get me started on how hard it is to dress for weather like that. Outside you need at least ten layers of clothing and may as well jump into a sleeping bag or two for good measure. Then, BOOM,

I'M NOT A MORNING PERSON

the minute you step inside the school it's summer in the tropics and you're forced to strip down, layer by layer, trying and failing to stuff everything into your locker as the day goes on.

Eventually, it got to the point where I was given a choice to stop my Instagram and pick up my grades or be sent home. I had

I wasn't kidding when I said the driveway was long!

originally planned to be in the United States for a year and I had been there for almost six months. I realized that six months was enough of an adventure. A lot of students only do exchanges for that amount of time, and looking back, I don't regret for a second deciding not to give up the Instagram account I had worked so hard to build.

The six months I had in the United States were life changing. I had traveled to San Francisco, New York, Chicago, Boston, Michigan, Las Vegas, and my personal favorite, Los Angeles. I had made lifelong friends and had a whole new family I continue to love like my own. For anyone reading this who is looking for a change or an adventure they'll never forget, I completely, 100 percent recommend giving a high school exchange a go.

As I boarded my flight back home to New Zealand I knew I had made the right decision to chase my passion and dreams. I gazed out the window as I flew above and away from a beautiful, snow-covered city and woke up to the summery skies and blue sparkling water of my home country. Little did I know, a whole new adventure waited.

HOLLYWOOD

My Homeland and Beyond!

Home ♥

It was so nice to be home again. As much as I love the United States, it's very fast paced and I happily welcomed the laid-back culture of New Zealand with open arms. The last few months had been such a crazy whirlwind, and it finally felt like I could breathe again.

I unpacked my suitcase into my old familiar bedroom and started settling back into normal life. I spent a few days recovering from jet lag and laying low, and then got in contact with some old friends from school. When we all got together to catch up, I was surprised to find that some of them almost seemed like different people, and the crazy part was that I couldn't figure out if they had changed or I had. They had these memories together that I had missed while I was away and I felt like I didn't fit in anymore. As they began talking about how exciting our last year of school was going to be my stomach dropped. I wasn't ready to go back.

This was playing on my mind, and one night my mom and I cuddled up on the couch with hot chocolates to talk about it. She agreed that I was in such a happy place that it would be a shame for me to go back there when we both knew it wouldn't turn out well. I decided I was old enough now and ready for university. I applied to a few and got accepted, and was even offered a scholarship to a design school in America. Although that was so tempting, I wasn't quite ready to fly halfway across the world again. We chose one close-by and found out that I had another six months to kill until my course started.

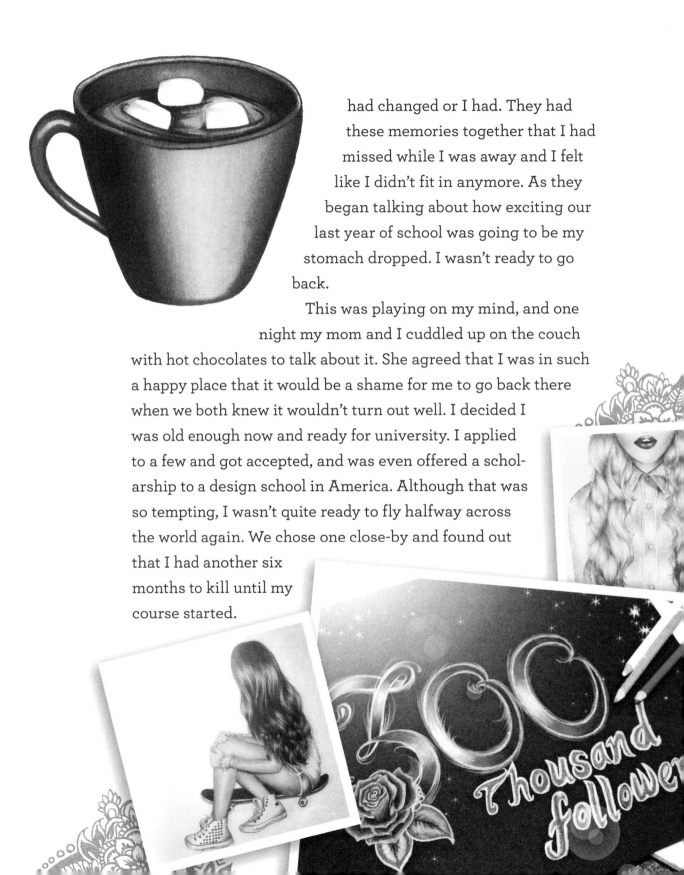

Not long after our talk I reached three hundred thousand followers and thought it was about time to introduce my mom to the wonderful world of Instagram. I remember showing it to her and being like, "This is my art, see," and "This is the number of people who see it." It was a completely foreign concept to her. I don't know about you guys and your moms, but mine is a little technology challenged. Clearly not understanding, she nodded along and smiled. One thing she did manage to understand though was just how happy it made me.

Unaware that Instagram was becoming a full-time job for me, my mom suggested it was time for me to get a "real" job. So while my old friends prepared for their first days as seniors, I was walking into the local shops and handing in résumés. Résumés, I might add, that stated I had zero work experience—so I wasn't holding my breath for any callbacks. My last stop was the local bakery, and funnily enough, the baker hired me on the spot.

I was now an official working professional and felt extremely grown-up and mature. I imagined my days would be filled with friendly small talk to customers and icing the occasional doughnut. Then reality hit me ... HARD.

Working wasn't easy! I was on my feet for hours on end, washing dishes, scraping trays, and sweeping floors. My shifts started so early it should be illegal and by the time I got home I could barely walk.

Even flopping down onto my bed was a mission. It was a good feeling though to be independent and earning money. I enjoyed it more as I got to know my workmates, who taught me how to use the till (cash register). And it turned out that my imagination wasn't completely wrong, as I became the official doughnut decorator. I was working full-time and with each week that went by I grew more and more exhausted.

One morning I woke up to the single most annoying sound in the world: my alarm. Groaning, I reached over to hit snooze, except something wasn't quite right. My arm wasn't working? *It's okay*, I told myself. *You just must have slept on it funny*. But after a few minutes I still had no control over it. It was like my brain was instructing it to do something and my arm was being a stubborn teenager. In a state of panic I jumped out of bed and the floor met my face. As I was recovering from the unintended face-plant my vision started going blurry and I couldn't see my room anymore. Yep, something was seriously wrong. Then the dreaded nausea hit.

I spent three days in the hospital and was told my body wasn't coping. I was run-down, overexhausted, and to top it off, had a bad case of glandular fever. That led to tonsillitis, which made it hard to breathe and was unbearably painful when I threw up from the migraines I was also having. I was one sick girl.

When I got released from the hospital I was on strict instructions to take it easy and spent a lot of time lying on the floor in a burrito of blankets and pillows with a good audiobook playing and a sketchpad in front of me. Drawing was my medicine,

My first
talk show!

and even once I had fully recovered, I never ended up returning
to the bakery. The time it had taken me to get better was the first
time in my life I had been able to focus purely on my Instagram,
and it began to grow in the thousands of followers every day. Now
that I was dedicating my full attention and time to creating art,
everything suddenly seemed to fit into place. My mom stood back
in amazement as she watched me do things I never dreamed of
doing—from magazine and newspaper articles to live radio and
television shows. Six months passed and I never ended up going
to that university course. Instead, I took the risk of seeing where
my art would lead me. I had no idea where it would take me or
how far, but I couldn't give up on it, not now.

The day I hit one million followers on my art account was a

Tauranga's internet sensation

Teen draws 400,000 internet fans

INSTA-ART

BE CREATIVE

KRISTINA WEBB
17, artist and Instagram phenomenon

Picture perfect

day I'll always remember. I couldn't fathom that amount of people. I never in my wildest dreams imagined so many people would come across what I created and actually like what they saw. I was overwhelmingly grateful and so thankful. Every single one of those people, even though they may not know it, has encouraged and supported me through this insane roller-coaster journey. Every single one of them has played a part in making my dreams come true.

And a big thank-you to you, the special person holding this book right now and reading these very words. This book you're holding is a dream I've had since I was a little girl sitting on my bed in Vanuatu staring adoringly at the illustrations in my favorite fairy tales and hoping that one day there would be someone looking at my artwork the same way I looked at those magical pages.

Something I never pictured though was that I'd be the author of that book and the book would be partly about me. When my publisher told me they wanted WORDS in here—WORDS about MY LIFE—I questioned whether I could do it. I'll be the first to admit that I haven't had any professional training to do this, but I challenged myself and gave it my best shot. It took being thrown out of my comfort zone to realize that, weirdly enough, even though I found it hard to write about myself, overall I've ended up really enjoying sharing my story. My hope is that you guys enjoy reading it too.

So now you know how I made it to this point. I certainly never dreamed that the Instagram account I had started on my seventeenth birthday in the United States would take me full circle back to the United States, but that's where I landed. The next part of my journey is still to be written. That's enough about me though. Now it's all about you. From now on this is YOUR book, YOUR story, and I can't wait to see YOUR art. Join me and create to inspire!

Dear Creatives,

Let me start by saying just how thankful and excited I am that you're joining me on this artistic adventure! I truly hope you have as much fun completing this book as I did creating it.

Now, down to the serious stuff. While you're completing this book, I only have one rule: there are no rules! Forget everything you learned in art class. This is about creating your own vision, your own style, and expressing yourself through the following pages in whichever way suits you best. There are no deadlines and, better yet, no one is grading you. In fact, you all pass with flying colors simply for giving it a try! So this is a perfect place to just let loose and let that crazy imagination of yours run wild.

Speaking of imagination: as kids we all had it in bucket loads. Often, however, reality kicks in and we are told to "grow up." Well, I'm asking you guys to grow back down. If you feel you've lost touch with your imagination, it's okay, you can get it back! This is something you can't simply learn by sitting in a classroom or reading yet another textbook. The ability to see beyond the usual can only come from hands-on experience.

Some of these challenges will ask you to put away the pencils and instead rummage through your room to find everyday things (a deck of playing cards, nail polish, candy wrappers, etc.) to turn something ordinary into the extraordinary. Not only that, but you will also play the part of an inventor, as you're asked to create things that don't yet exist.

As far as completing this book, just do it whenever or wherever you please. Inspiration can't be forced, and you never know when it will strike. Try and find your own "happy place." For me, I throw a million blankets and pillows on the floor, grab a sketchbook, and lie down to draw. Oh, and of course, good snacks—can't forget the snacks!

The challenges I've come up with are designed to help and inspire you, but the last thing I ever want to do is restrict you. Remember, this is your journey, so do whatever feels right. Please don't get frustrated or stressed out. If you're struggling on a certain page or just having a bad day, it's easy to begin doubting your artwork. Don't let it get the better of you: put down the book, take some time away, and come back to it later when you feel refreshed. Or if you think you've made a mistake, don't stress about it. My mom always taught me that everything is fixable.

That black smudge of paint you accidentally got on your artwork? No worries! Just turn it into a random bird flying across the page.

I can't wait to see all your creations on various social media. Use #cmcbook so I can start stalking your accounts and possibly repost your work. Art is a constant chain of inspiration from one person to another. Who knows what your artwork could inspire somebody else to create?

So, are you up for the challenge? Or should I say challenges?

Just remember, the most important thing is to have fun. Love you all and good luck!

Kristina Webb

Warm-Up Challenges

Signature Challenge

When I was around fifteen years old I did the 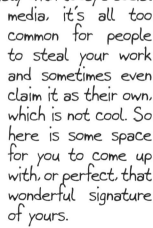 drawing below and uploaded it to my Tumblr account. This was nothing unusual, but the next morning I went online to discover it had gotten hundreds of thousands of notes and had gone internet viral. I couldn't believe it—my art was being seen by more people than I ever imagined! There was just one problem: no one knew it was mine. In my rush to upload the drawing I had forgotten to sign it. I began seeing it everywhere: on Facebook, websites, even hanging up in people's homes or businesses. I made a big mistake—a mistake I don't want any of you lovely people to make.

One of the most important pieces of advice I can give you is to make sure everyone knows it's *your* work. Sign every single creation you put out into the world. You never know how popular it could be or where it might end up. Especially with today's social media, it's all too common for people to steal your work and sometimes even claim it as their own, which is not cool. So here is some space for you to come up with, or perfect, that wonderful signature of yours.

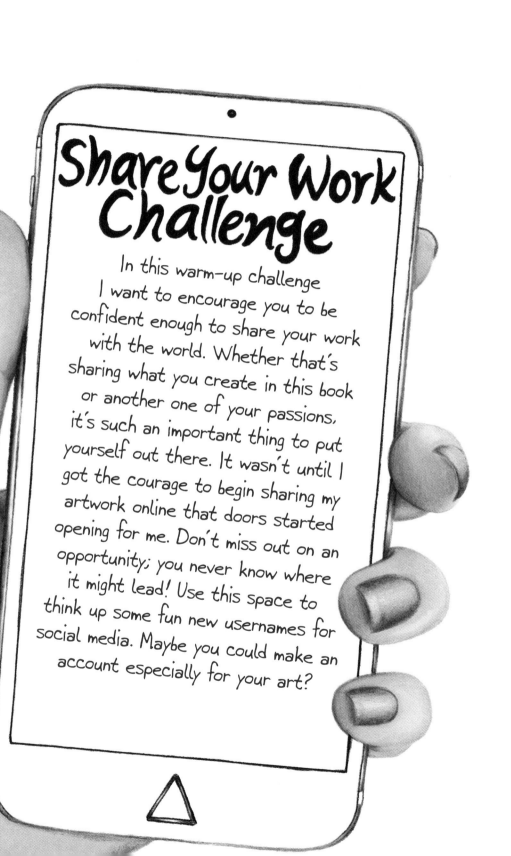

Share Your Work Challenge

In this warm-up challenge I want to encourage you to be confident enough to share your work with the world. Whether that's sharing what you create in this book or another one of your passions, it's such an important thing to put yourself out there. It wasn't until I got the courage to begin sharing my artwork online that doors started opening for me. Don't miss out on an opportunity; you never know where it might lead! Use this space to think up some fun new usernames for social media. Maybe you could make an account especially for your art?

Stay Positive Challenge

If you have set up a social media account or are sharing your artwork with the online world, then I have to warn you: anyone who puts themselves out there is going to receive a negative comment or two every so often. I have personally had to deal with this, and I've dealt with it in many different ways over the years. My best advice is, "Ignore and Delete." Realize that you have full control over what happens on YOUR account, so use those delete and block buttons, because you have all the power. If you respond in any way you are giving them exactly what they want—attention—and not only that, but also your precious time. Most important, learn to focus on the positive comments you get! The ones that encourage you, support you, and make you smile. Sometimes you might get a comment that just makes your day. When that happens, write it here! This is a page for encouragements, a page of support and love. You can pass this book around and get people to write nice little things in this area or just make a big collage of positivity. That way, when you get down, doubt yourself, or see someone say something that's hurtful, you can turn back to this page full of lovely comments, the comments that actually matter.

ART
IDEAS
CHALLENGE...

How many times have you come up with a brilliant idea, forgotten to write it down, and then not been able to remember it later? Countless times? Well, don't you worry, this page is here to save the day. While completing this book you may suddenly come up with an awesome art idea of your own, and if that happens, here is the place to quickly write it down.

Write your ideas on these lines!
(Add more if you need to.)

COVER CHALLENGE

This book is now all about YOU and YOUR artwork, so it's only fitting that you design your own cover for it. Use the page to the right to create your new cover. Stick on photos of you, doodle all over it, throw glitter everywhere—whatever you feel like doing to make it unique and fun and something you're happy to look at! Then paste your new cover right on the front of this book—don't forget to include the book's title, *Color Me Creative*! If you want to, share your new personalized cover with the world and hashtag it to #cmcbook.

COLOR ME CREATIVE

Challenges

Awesome! Now you've completed these warm-up challenges it's time to really let your imagination run wild! Have fun!! xx

Colored Pencils Challenge

Draw your own
creative designs coming
out of the pencils on
the right-hand page.

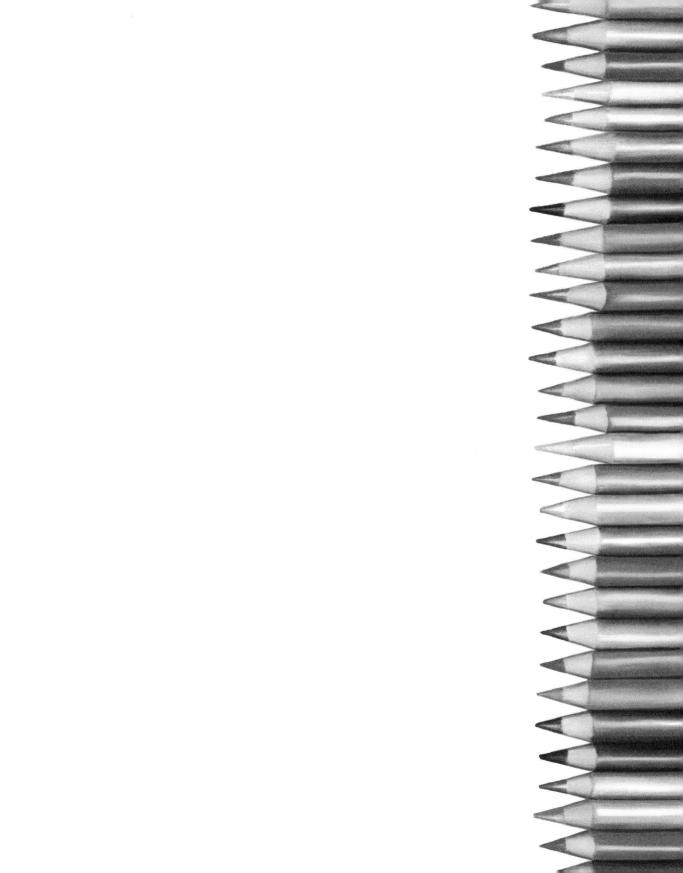

eyechallenge

Fill in the blank page
to your right with every kind
of eye imaginable (think: different
shapes, colors, sizes). Perhaps
cartoon eyes, celebrity eyes, your
eyes, animal eyes . . . you name it,
draw their eyes!

CREATE A FRUIT
CHALLENGE

Okay, so on the right is a branch. Imagine the craziest-looking fruit possible hanging from it. Have you got something in mind? Okay, now draw it! Oh, and don't forget to give it an equally crazy name!

DOODLE CHALLENGE

While watching television, listening to music, or doing a mindless activity, I want you to doodle all over the page to your right. You don't have to complete it all in one go; just keep returning to this page until it is completely covered.

120

Emoji Challenge

I think almost everyone has had a moment when they are sending a text to their friend and wish that a certain emoji existed. Well, here's your chance! In the boxes to the right, draw and design the emojis that you think should most definitely exist.

Fix It Up Challenge

Are you right-handed or left-handed?
Okay, now pick up a pencil with your weaker hand
and draw the first thing that comes into your
head. Have a good laugh about your "masterpiece."
Then, pick up another pencil (different color)
with your dominant hand and do your best to fix
up your drawing to make whatever you just drew
beautiful. The message behind this challenge is
that no matter what mistakes you make in art,
everything is always fixable. You just have
to use your imagination.

Dream Wardrobe Challenge

Have you ever seen
an item of clothing and
wished it would just magically
appear in your wardrobe?
I certainly have. Design three
pieces of clothing that you
wish were hanging in
your closet right now!

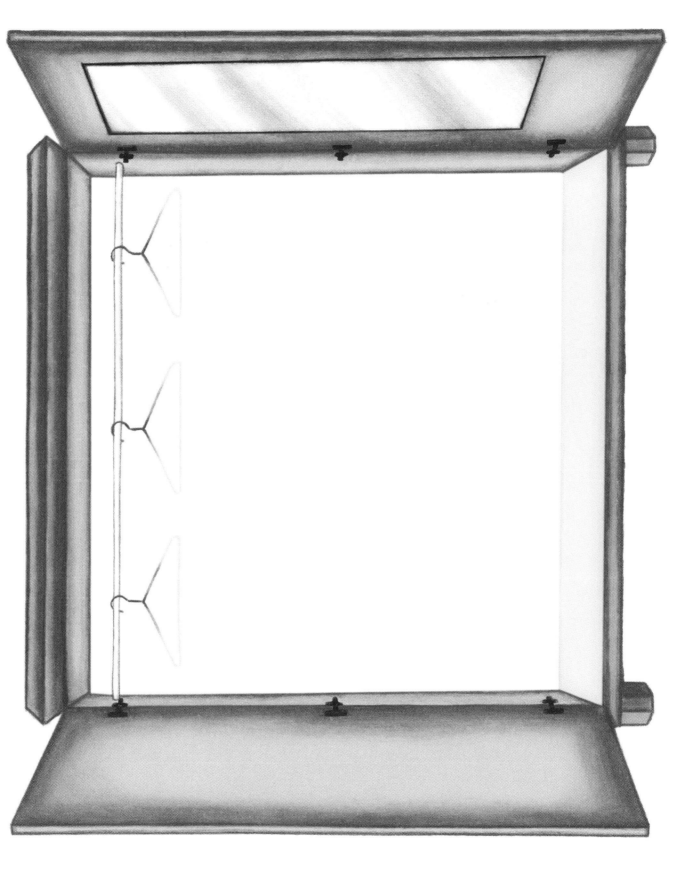

FUTURE CHALLENGE

Welcome to the future! Look around you and find an object or item you use every day (a car, a hair dryer, a computer). Now on the right-hand page draw what you think that thing will look like a hundred years from now!

Inch by Inch Challenge

Details, details, details! Practice drawing on
a smaller scale by filling in each inch-by-inch
square with a different tiny image every day.
Or you can just do them all in one go;
you're the one in control here.

Dream Pet Challenge

Invent your dream pet—real, imaginary, or a combination of many animals! Oh, and you can't create a pet without giving it a name!

Henna Challenge

Be inspired by
traditional henna and
create your own unique
designs on these hands.

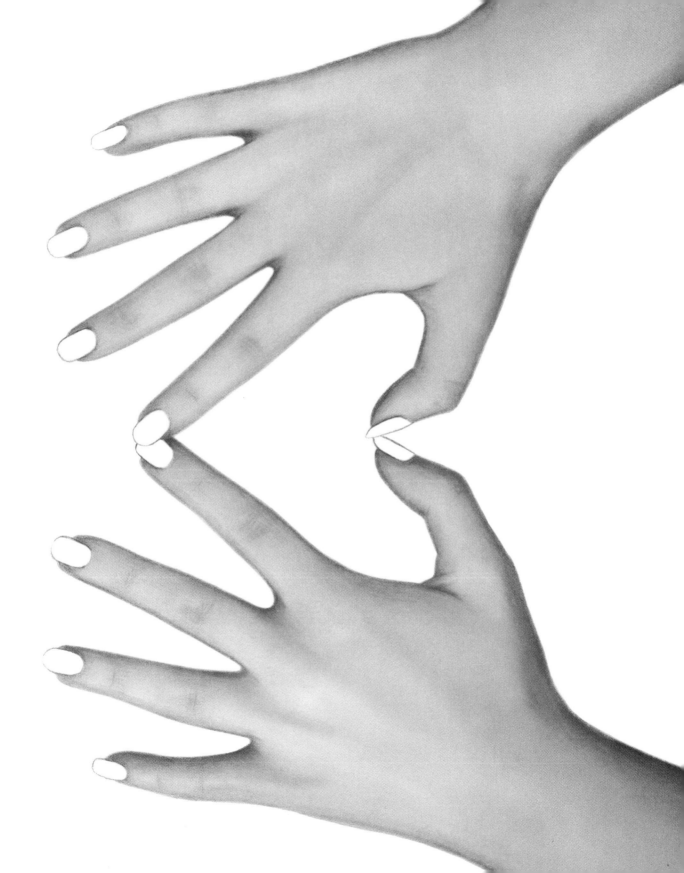

Watercolor Challenge

It's time to make a beautiful mess—
with watercolors! Paint lines, swirls,
and curls everywhere.
Before it all dries, find a straw
and blow through it onto your
colorful creation to make
the paint run and drip colors in
every direction.

Headdress Challenge

Finish off the drawing of this girl and give her something fun on the top of her head. A flower wreath, perhaps, or a beautiful crown? A massive bow? Maybe even animal ears. Whatever you decide, just have fun with it.

Scribble Challenge

This is going to be a real test of your imagination. I want you to make the scribbles I drew to the right into something. A person? An animal? Think randomly, the first thing you see when you look at these scribbles; just go with it.

Make the cupcake to your right the yummiest, most fabulous-looking cupcake you can dream up.

Changing Color Challenge

Grab a handful
of colored pencils, pick one up,
and draw whatever you feel like,
but every time your pencil leaves
the page, pick up a new color to
continue your creation
and so on.

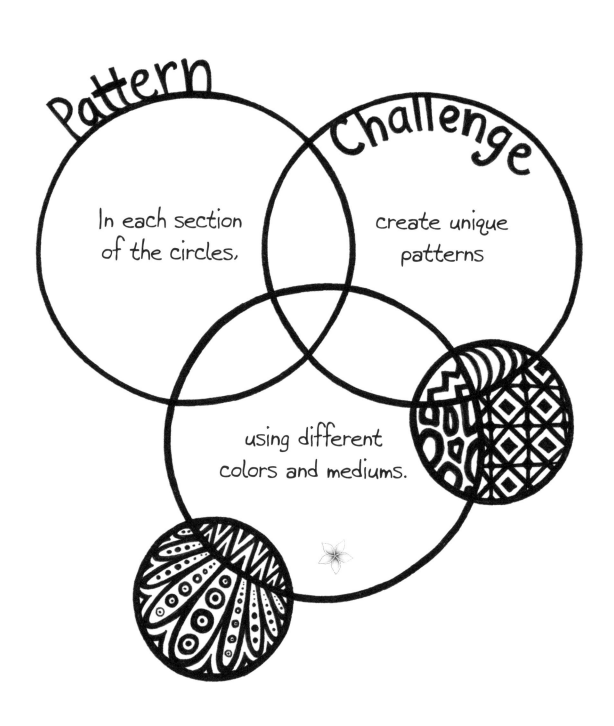

Pattern

Challenge

In each section of the circles,

create unique patterns

using different colors and mediums.

Photo Continued Challenge

Forget boundaries!
Stick a photo on the right-hand
page and continue the image
beyond the photo's borders.

Bedroom Wall Challenge

I feel like almost everyone has had the urge to draw on the walls at some point in their lives. Unfortunately, for most of us this just isn't an option. Well, here is your chance. Pretend this next page is your bedroom wall and decorate it however you want.

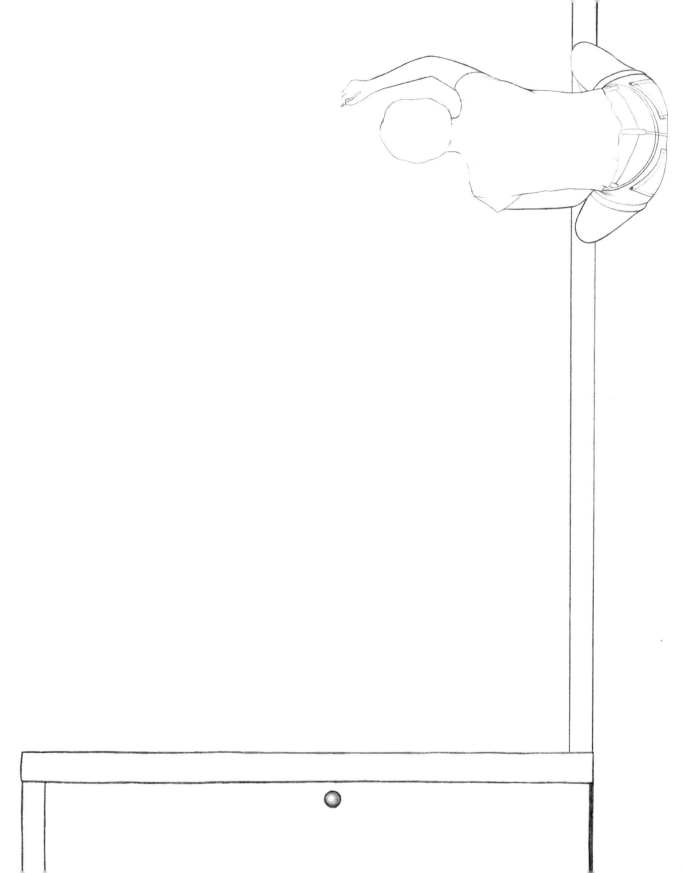

High5Challenge

Throwing it back to toddler days, paint a design on your hand and before it dries give a decent high five to the page on your right (meaning hit the page as hard as you can). You'll end up with an interesting handprint painting. It's like a more advanced version of the handprints you probably did as a kid.

Hair Goals Challenge

The silhouettes to your right are all about hair goals. Try drawing hairstyles, bright colors, or complicated hairdos you've always wanted to try or just simply like the look of.

Eraser Challenge

Cover the entire page lightly with lead pencil. When finished, use only your eraser to create a picture. What you'll end up with is basically a reverse drawing.

Face Paint Challenge

What's the craziest face paint you can imagine? A tiger mask? A Halloween-worthy vampire? It's time to practice your face-painting skills. Get those paintbrushes out and create the look on the face to your right. Afterward if you are feeling brave I dare you to try to re-create your design on someone's actual face.

Tattoo Challenge

Tattoos are the most personal form of art! Become a tattoo artist for a little while and draw tattoos on the people on the right-hand page.

Masked Ball Challenge

Imagine you were just invited to a masquerade ball! Using paint, pencils, feathers, glitter, or anything else you wish, create your dream mask on this template. Afterward, feel free to cut it out and take a selfie in your fabulous mask. (Keep in mind that cutting out your mask will interfere with the Frame Challenge instructions on the next page, so make sure to read those first. ☺)

frame Challenge

Glue one of your favorite photos on top of the dotted rectangle to your right. Now design the most extravagant frame you can think up.

Favorites Challenge

This challenge is about you, more specifically about your faves. Cover every inch of these two pages with all your favorite things: food, movies, sports, flowers, colors, musicians, and anything else you can possibly think of. You can write out the words or draw images or a combination of both!

Superhero Challenge

I think I can safely say that everyone has dreamed they were a superhero at one point. Well, here's your chance to save the world! Draw yourself in your dream hero costume. Don't forget to give yourself a superpower and a superawesome name!

NAIL ART CHALLENGE

Create different nail art ideas to try later on your actual fingernails. Feeling fancy? Try using real nail polish on the page!

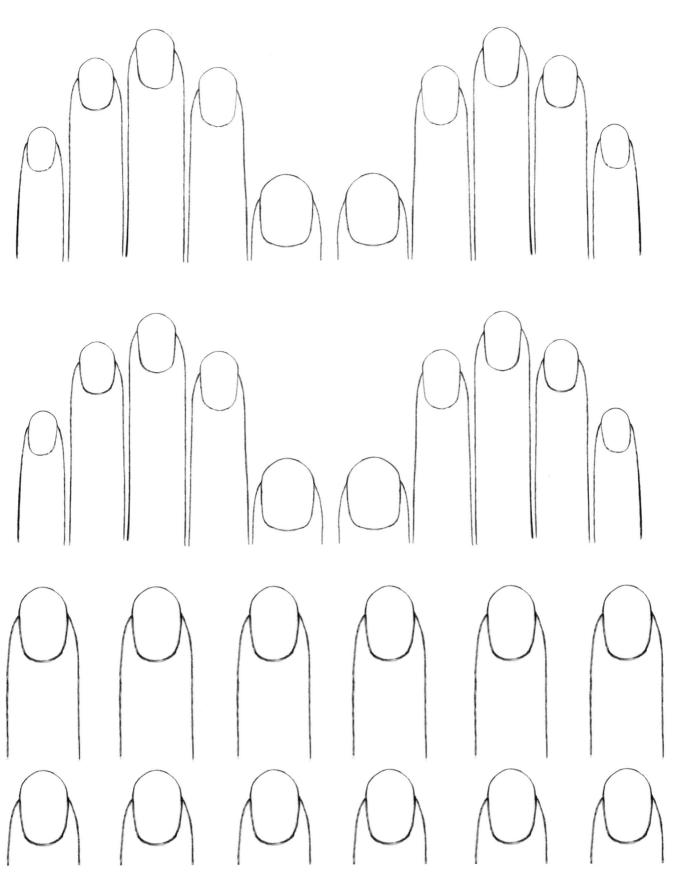

Don't you love getting lost in a good book? On the right-hand page, make a list of your favorite books. Then choose one and turn the page. Think about how you would have designed the cover of your favorite book.

BOOKLOVERCHALLENGE

Next, try drawing your favorite character. How did you imagine him or her to look while you were first reading the book?

MY TOP 5 BOOKS

1.

2.

3.

4.

5.

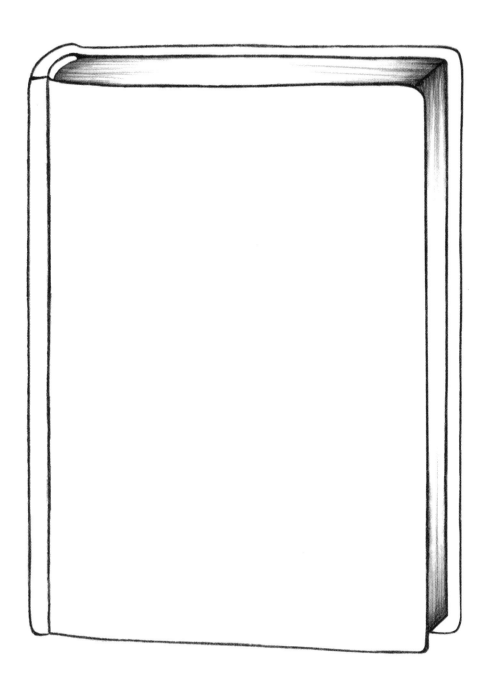

missing Piece Challenge

Choose a photo of yours or a picture from a magazine. Cut out a section or piece of the image, discard that piece, and then paste the rest of the image on the right-hand page. Using your imagination, fill in the blank space.

GIVE BACK CHALLENGE

Write and design inspirational quotes or sayings inside each of the rectangles on the right. Once finished, cut them out and try to sneak them individually to people you know could use some encouragement at the moment, a little something to make their day better. You can write your name on it if you want or leave it anonymously. Small gestures of kindness can mean a lot to people.

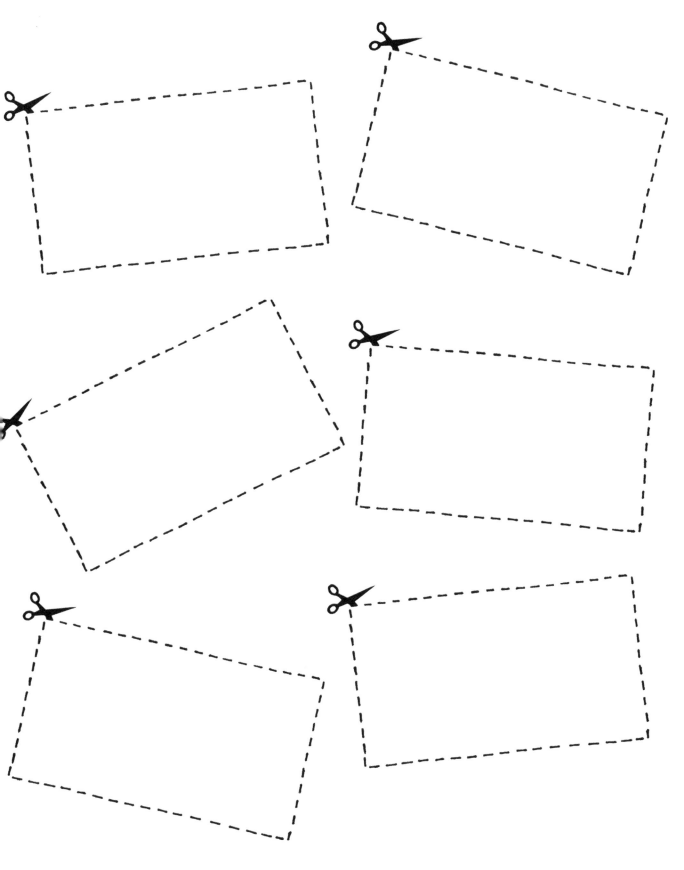

Make sure to decorate the backs!

WINDOW CHALLENGE

If you could see anything through this window, what would it be? Cut out the center and design, draw, or paste your perfect view on the next page.

Draw or paste your view on this page

Magazine Makeover Challenge

Re-face or De-face? Flip through the pages of a magazine of your choice and find a picture of someone you feel could use some of your artistic flair.

Grab your permanent markers, paints, and pens and give the image a complete makeover (think crazy makeup, tattoos, freckles, colorful hair, etc.). Once finished, rip out the page and paste it on the right-hand page.

I'm going to challenge you to look at the world in a different way. You're going to create a planet. Think colors, patterns, mountains, and oceans. It's your planet; do what you feel like. Maybe put a ring on it? At the end, because you invented the planet, you should probably give it an equally cool name.

PLANET CHALLENGE

DRESS
Design Challenge

You are now officially a fashion designer. Create
a dress using anything out of the ordinary. Here
is a list of examples:
- flower petals
- playing cards
- pencil shavings
- lettuce
- sequins
- leaves
- candy wrappers

Or come up with something totally
out of the blue; the sky's the limit!

See some of my ideas!

COFFEE CUP
CHALLENGE

Get a paper cup or napkin from a coffee shop. Find a way to decorate one or both of these items to make them less ordinary! Tape the finished napkin and/or a photo of your reimagined coffee cup on the page to your right.

It's
okay;
everyone
has a little bit
of inner stalker
in them. I want you to
draw the face of a total stranger.
It could be someone you spot at a coffee shop,
on the bus, or in the library. Just try not to get
caught, because that could be potentially awkward!
If that does happen, just show the lovely stranger
these instructions and I'll happily let you blame the
crazy person who wrote this book.

FABRIC CHALLENGE

Sew a piece of fabric onto the next page where the dotted rectangle is. Once it's attached, use fabric markers or fabric paint to create designs on the material. If you found it fun, find an old T-shirt or a pillow lying around and continue creating.

inspiration challenge

Draw someone who has inspired
you in some way—someone who made a
lasting impact on your life and who you look
up to as a role model. It might be a friend,
family member, celebrity, or really anyone
who fits that description. If you can, let
them know how much they mean to you by
showing them your finished drawing.

Petal Challenge

Picture that each of these circles is the center of a flower. Draw and design unique petals to create new types of flowers that exist only in your imagination.

Therapy Challenge

Use your feelings and emotions to create art. Whether you're sad, happy, or angry, write down your feelings and use the words to create a piece of art. Not only is it a wonderful way to express yourself, it's also really therapeutic to get your feelings out in the open instead of keeping them all bottled up inside.

Butterfly Wing Challenge

I've drawn the middle of the butterfly and now it's your turn to create the wings. Not just normal wings either—invent your own species of butterfly and give this butterfly wings like no other.

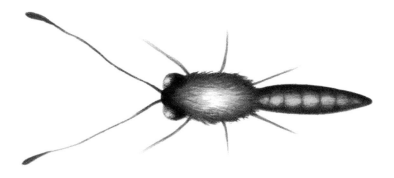

Creating for a Cause Challenge

Use this page to express something close to your heart: antibullying, cancer awareness, protesting animal cruelty, etc. Your art is your voice; use it to stand up for something you believe in.

Challenge Yourself Challenge

Now it's your turn! This challenge is to challenge yourself to design your own unique challenge and complete it. Sound challenging? (Have I used the word *challenge* enough?☺) When you're finished, post your creation and your instructions on various social media using #cmcbook and maybe you'll inspire other creatives, including myself, to have a go at your challenge!

Use this page to brainstorm ideas, and then turn the page to design your final challenge.

Acknowledgments

A huge thank-you to:

. . . once again, my incredible followers for making all this possible. I know I have already dedicated this book to you all, but I can just never thank you wonderful people enough.

. . . my mom, Jan, who from that day in Vanuatu when she first put a pencil in my two-year-old hand has never stopped believing in me and my art and has allowed me to follow my own path in life. Thank you for keeping me sane during the tight deadline of this book and for keeping the fridge supplied with chocolate for when things got too stressful. How can I put into words everything that I am thankful to you for in one paragraph when you deserve an entire book? You always go above and beyond and inspire me to be better every day.

Mom

211

. . . my sister, Rochelle, who has always encouraged me to think big and step outside my comfort zone. We're sisters, so naturally we bring out each other's "crazy" every now and then, but after a few hours we'll undoubtedly be cuddling up and having a good giggle about how silly we are. You're not only my sister, but also my partner in crime, my travel buddy, my opposite in almost every way, and most important, my best friend. Oh, and thanks for letting me tell stories and share funny, embarrassing photos/videos of you torturing me as a kid. I suppose you didn't have a lot of choice. Finally got my payback!

. . . my nan and pop for being my rocks and my role models and giving the best hugs in the world. Thank you to my pop for stepping in and being the most wonderful father figure for both my sister and me to look up to. To both of you for your endless support,

Nan and Pop

interest, and excitement in every success, big or small, that I have accomplished. And also for caring enough to learn how to use an iPad at over eighty years old to follow my online journey. Mom, Rochelle, and I love you both unconditionally; you've shaped us all into the people we are now and for that we are forever grateful.

... the team at HarperCollins, especially my lovely editor, Nancy Inteli, and her assistant editor, Nicole Hoff, for always being enthusiastic and open to my ideas! For letting me be me and gently guiding me through this scary process of writing my first book.

... my literary agent, Matthew Elblonk, whose humor and encouragement helped put my sister and me at ease in the publishing world, guiding us around New York City and taking on the bad karma of accidentally stealing someone's yellow taxi to get us to a meeting on time. :)

... to Max Stubblefield, my agent, who is incredible at what he does and believed in me and my dreams from the minute we first met. He often tells me that I bring out his creative side, so I'm expecting you to give this book a try, Max!

Even though you have now come to the end of this book, it doesn't mean it's the end of your artistic journey. Keep challenging yourself and expressing your inner creative.